Obento

Snack Pack 1

Sue Xouris

NELSON
CENGAGE Learning™

Australia • Brazil • Japan • Korea • Mexico • Singapore • Spain • United Kingdom • United States

Obento Snack Pack 1
1st Edition
Sue Xouris

Editors: Yoshi Abe, Rani Kellock, Craig Metcher
Publishing editor: Margherita Ghezzi
Senior Designer: Vonda Pestana
Text designer: Yuri Tanabe
Typesetter: Yuri Tanabe
Text illustrator: U-Suke
Cover designer: Vonda Pestana
Photo research: Corrina Tauschke
Production controller: Hanako Smith
Typeset in Kyokashotai and Gill Sans by Yuri Tanabe

For product information and technology assistance,
in Australia call 1300 790 853;
in New Zealand call 0508 635 766

For permission to use material from this text or product,
please email **aust.permissions@cengage.com**

National Library of Australia Cataloguing-in-Publication Data
Xouris, Sue
Obento Snack Pack 1

For secondary school age
ISBN 978 0 17 013543 6

Japanese Language - Textbooks.

495.682421

Cengage Learning Australia
Level 7, 80 Dorcas Street
South Mebourne, Victoria Australia 3205

Cengage Learning New Zealand
Unit 4B Rosedale Office Park
331 Rosedale Road, Albany, North Shore 0632, NZ

For learning solutions, visit **cengage.com.au**

Printed in Australia by Ligare Pty Ltd
14 15 16 17 18 19 20 21 20 19 18 17

Contents

indicates you need the teacher's CD ROM to complete this task

suggests you to check out the Internet for more information and resources

indicates your teacher has extra material for you to complete this task

indicates this is a game to play in class [the teacher may have extra instructions and worksheets]

①あいさつ

Greetings

How do you greet your friend? How do you greet your teacher? How do you greet your little brother? OK, let's not go there!! Let's talk about how people greet each other and learn how to say hello and goodbye to your family, your teacher and friends at different times of the day … in Japanese. Take a minute to navigate the page and guess what it's all about, then check out the CD-ROM.

NEW STUFF きょうのポイント

Practise these new words on the CD-ROM, and then fill in the English meanings.

おはようございます
o ha yo u go za i ma su ______________________

こんにちは
ko n ni chi wa ______________________

さようなら
sa yo u na ra ______________________

またあした
ma ta a shi ta ______________________

おやすみなさい
o ya su mi na sa i ______________________

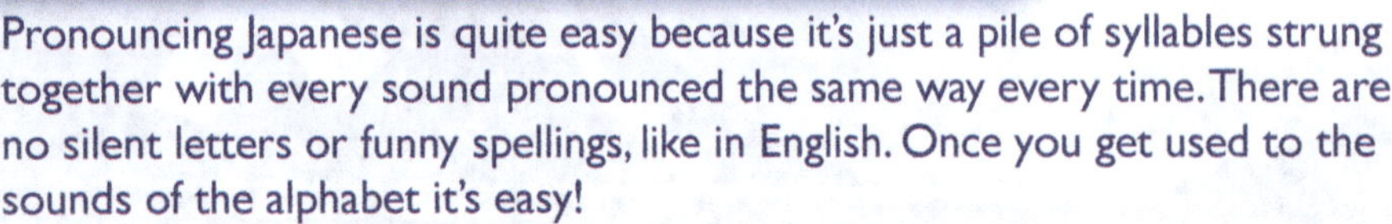

Here's how you say it!

Pronouncing Japanese is quite easy because it's just a pile of syllables strung together with every sound pronounced the same way every time. There are no silent letters or funny spellings, like in English. Once you get used to the sounds of the alphabet it's easy!

You'll notice we have spelt the words out in English letters underneath the Japanese, so that you'll know how to pronounce them. Notice how there is usually a vowel or a consonant followed by a vowel? That's because each of the Japanese characters is made up of those sounds. If you are having trouble pronouncing a word it helps if you split it up into its syllables. o-ha-yo-u-go-za-i-ma-su. You can say it slowly first, then bring it up to speed.

What are they saying?

Watch the skits on the CD-ROM and number the greeting you hear.

GOOD MORNING

GOOD AFTERNOON

SEE YOU TOMORROW

GOODBYE

GOODNIGHT

Match and Colour

Draw a line matching the picture with the correct expression. (Use the New Stuff section to help you.) Then colour the picture frame and the word box blue if it is a "hello" expression and red if it is a "goodbye" expression.

おやすみなさい

さようなら

こんにちは

Listen to the song on the CD-ROM, and then sing along!

ド・レ・ミ・ファ・そんぐ

The greetings song to the tune of *The Farmer in the Dell*

O ha yo u go za i ma su, O ha yo go za i ma su
It's what you say to start the day
O ha yo u go za i ma su

Ko n ni chi wa, Ko n ni chi wa,
You see your friend, it's after 10
Ko n ni chi wa

Ma ta a shi ta, Ma ta a shi ta
Got to go, see you tomorrow
Ma ta a shi ta

Sa yo u na ra, Sa yo u na ra
Goodbye, goodbye, we've got to fly
Sa yo u na ra

O ya su mi na sa i, O ya su mi na sa i
It's all been said, I'm going to bed.

Make an Origami Finger Puppet!

Check out our CD-ROM to make an origami finger puppet. Then give your puppet a Japanese name and, using your finger puppet as a character, have a conversation in Japanese with your friend's puppet.

日本では...

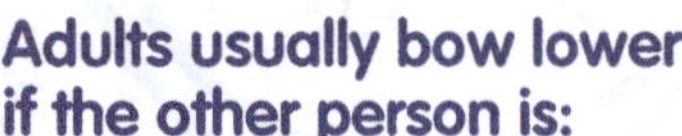

IN JAPAN

When Japanese people meet each other they usually:
a) wave
b) shake hands
c) bow
d) wink

Adults usually bow lower if the other person is:
a) taller than them
b) higher in status than them
c) shorter than them
d) prettier than them

Younger people like you may simply greet friends by:
a) shouting their names out loud
b) winking
c) nodding
c) shaking hands

Talk Time おしゃべりタイム

Grab a friend!
Role-play these scenarios in Japanese.

It's 6 o'clock in the morning. Your mum wakes you up with a far too cheerful "good morning." You answer her with an annoyed, "Mum!" She tries again, "Good Morning." You answer her reluctantly, "Good Morning."

It's lunchtime. Your friend calls out to you across the playground. You don't hear. They call out again. You turn around and call. "Oh! Hi (insert name here)!" They say hello to you. You both start walking to class. Three other friends appear. You say hello to them. Your teacher appears, and you all greet him/her.

Now try to make up senarios where you use the words: sayonara, mata ashita and oyasumi nasai.

XTRA STUFF もっともっと

Check out the CD-ROM for some extra stuff that you can use when talking to your family and friends.

おかあさん o ka a sa n	Mum
おとうさん o to u sa n	Dad
さん sa n	used after people's names
くん ku n	used after young boys' names
ちゃん cha n	used after children's names
せんせい se n se i	used after teachers' names

If you are saying someone's name as you greet them, put the name first.

E.g. おかあさん、おやすみなさい。
o ka a sa n o ya su mi na sa i

Good night mum.

It's your turn!

- Say good morning to your mum.
- Say good night to your dad.
- Say good afternoon to your teacher.
- Say see you tomorrow to your friend, Jack.
- Say goodbye to your little sister, Holly.

X CROSS WORD

1	(blank)
2	S
3	S
4	(blank)
5	O
6	S
7	O
8	C
9	(blank)
10	M

よこ Across

1 ______________ said after young boys' names
4 ______________ good morning
7 ______________ good night
9 ______________ Dad
10 ______________ See you tomorrow

たて Down

1 ______________ hello
2 ______________ goodbye
3 ______________ said after people's names
5 ______________ Mum
6 ______________ said after teachers' names
8 ______________ said after children's names

しゅくだい HOMEWORK:

Say good morning and goodnight to all of the members of your family every day for one week. See how long it takes them to answer you correctly. Which family member was the first to get it?

CD ROM Hey! I can:

- ☐ Say hello and goodbye to my friends and family
- ☐ Say hello and goodbye to my teacher
- ☐ Talk about some Japanese customs of greeting

Milly's Afternoon Snack
ミリーちゃんのおやつ

When Milly came home from school she was hungry.
がっこうからかえって、ミリーちゃんはおなかがすいた。

So she ate one sushi roll.
だから、すしを一つ食べた。

But, she was still hungry
でも、まだおなかがすいたから

so she ate 2 yakitori sticks
やきとりを二つ食べた。

But, she was still hungry
でも、まだおなかがすいたから

so she ate 3 hamburgers. **ハンバーガーを三つ食べた。**

But, she was still hungry.
でも、まだおなかがすいたから

so she ate 4 rice-balls. **おにぎりを四つ食べた。**

But, she was still hungry
でも、まだおなかがすいたから

so she ate 5 bananas. **バナナを五つ食べた。**

But, she was still hungry
でも、まだおなかがすいたから
so she ate 6 apples.
りんごを六つ食べた。

But, she was still hungry
でも、まだおなかがすいたから
so she ate 7 doughnuts.
ドーナツを七つ食べた。

But, she was still hungry
でも、まだおなかがすいたから
so she ate 8 pancakes.
ホットケーキを八つ食べた。

But, she was still hungry
でも、まだおなかがすいたから
so she ate 9 chocolate icecreams.
チョコレート・アイスクリームを九つ食べた。

burp!
Finally, Milly was full.
とうとう、 ミリーはおなかがいっぱいになった。

When Ben came home from school he was hungry.
がっこうからかえって、ベンくんはおなかがすいた。
yum! pizza!
やったー!! ピザ!

②日本語のかきかた
Japanese writing

On this page you will learn all about Japanese writing. You'll learn how to read 5 characters and the 5 greetings that you already know. And that's not all! You will also read a book in Japanese!!!!!

Writing in Japanese

Three different writing systems are used together to write Japanese.

Hiragana お	Katakana オ	Kanji 日本
Look round and curly.	Look like straight lines with pointy bits.	Look like little pictures of what the word means.
One character, one sound.	One character, one sound.	Each character is like a word and means something.
There are 46 hiragana, but some of them can be turned into other sounds by adding ゛ or ゜.	There are 46 katakana, but some of them can be turned into other sounds by adding ゛ or ゜.	There are 1945 frequently used kanji which will enable you to read a newspaper and most books. However, you can write all Japanese by only using hiragana and katakana.
Used for writing Japanese words.	Used for writing words which come from other languages.	Used for writing Japanese words.

Japanese can be written downwards from right to left or across from left to right

Let's think about it!

1. What do the following words all have in common?

すし (su shi)　やきとり (ya ki to ri)　おにぎり (o ni gi ri)

2. What do the following words all have in common?

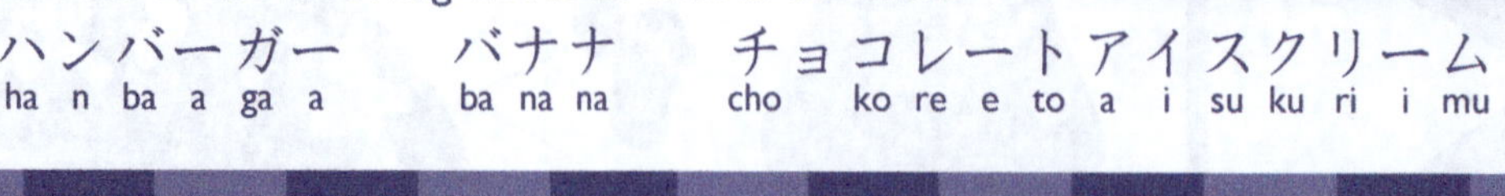

ハンバーガー (ha n ba a ga a)　バナナ (ba na na)　チョコレートアイスクリーム (cho ko re e to a i su ku ri i mu)

CD ROM

Ask your teacher to read you the story of ミリーちゃんのおやつ (*Milly's Afternoon Snack*, on pages 6 and 7). Then open up the CD-ROM and see how you can learn to read it yourself.

Colour!

Colour all the hiragana yellow.

Colour all the katakana orange.

Colour all the kanji green.

Recognize it!

See if you can find some examples of hiragana, katakana and kanji in *Milly's Afternoon Snack.* Think about the shapes of the characters and use the pictures to help you.

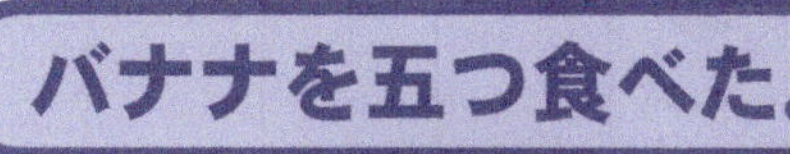

a) Find the word for sushi. It has 2 hiragana sounds. Su-shi. Circle it in green.

b) Find the word for yakitori. It has 4 hiragana sounds. Ya–ki-to-ri. Circle it in blue.

c) Find the word for hamburger. It has 6 katakana sounds. Ha-n-ba-a-ga-a. Circle it in blue.

d) Find the numbers 1, 2 and 3. Circle them in red.

e) Find the word for bananas. It has 3 katakana sounds. Ba-na-na. Circle it in yellow. Why is it written in katakana?

f) Find 5 examples of the kanji meaning "ate" Circle them in purple.

Beetle Battle

Check around the page for beetles and circle.

the お beetles red.

the こ beetles blue.

the さ beetles yellow.

the ま beetles green.

the や beetles orange.

A closer look at Hiragana

	w	r	y	m	h	n	t	s	k		
ん	わ	ら	や	ま	は	な	た	さ	か	あ	a
		り		み	ひ	に	ち	し	き	い	i
		る	ゆ	む	ふ	ぬ	つ	す	く	う	u
		れ		め	へ	ね	て	せ	け	え	e
	を	ろ	よ	も	ほ	の	と	そ	こ	お	o

かなコーナー Kana Corner

Now let's learn some to read and write some hiragana. Have your pencil ready and watch the video. Also refer to the hiragana table.

Practise writing the hiragana in the boxes provided.

o	お	お						
ko	こ	こ						
sa	さ	さ						
ma	ま	ま						
ya	や	や						

Greetings

Revise the greetings with your teacher, then see if you can read them. Join up the Japanese word with the English meaning, and then check the CD-ROM.

またあした •	• Good morning
おはようございます •	• Good afternoon
おやすみなさい •	• Goodbye
こんにちは •	• See you tomorrow
さようなら •	• Good night

Puzzle:

Link up each hiragana with its key word by colouring the character, the word and the correct path between them, all the same colour

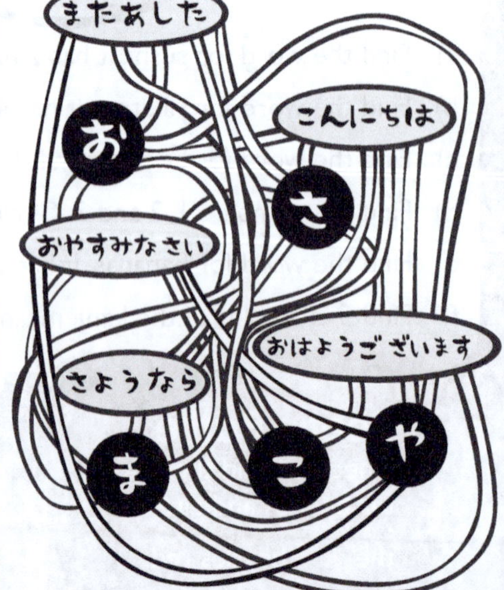

A closer look at Katakana

	w	r	y	m	h	n	t	s	k		
ン	ワ	ラ	ヤ	マ	ハ	ナ	タ	サ	カ	ア	a
		リ		ミ	ヒ	ニ	チ	シ	キ	イ	i
		ル	ユ	ム	フ	ヌ	ツ	ス	ク	ウ	u
		レ		メ	ヘ	ネ	テ	セ	ケ	エ	e
	ヲ	ロ	ヨ	モ	ホ	ノ	ト	ソ	コ	オ	o

Some more Katakana

Check out the katakana chart.

Listen to the CD-ROM and try to figure out the meanings of these words. Notice the character "ー". It doesn't have a sound of its own, but it's really useful because it makes the vowel sound before it a long sound.

1 ケーキ ____________

2 アイスクリーム ____________

3 ハンバーガー ____________

4 バナナ ____________

5 ピザ ____________

6 ドーナツ ____________

Listen up!

Listen to the CD-ROM and identify which of the items would be written in hiragana and which would be written in katakana. Remember when you use them, and check the table "Writing in Japanese" on page 8 if you need help. Write the item number in the appropriate box.

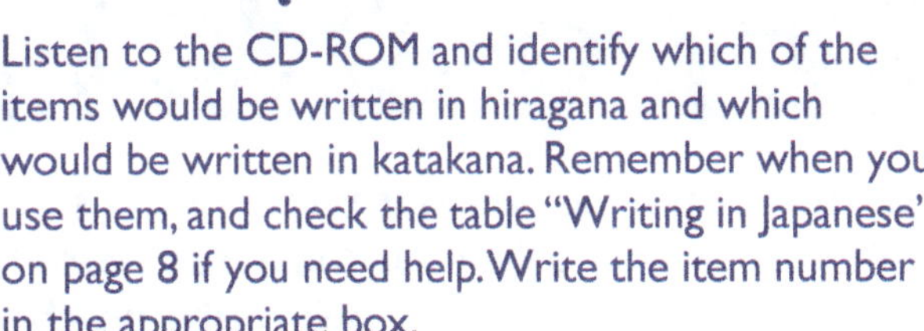

Hiragana	Katakana

Kanji!

Find out all about kanji on the CD-ROM, then try to guess the meanings of each of these from the pictures.

山____ 川____ 木____ 火____ 日____ 人____

Hey! Look at this! If you put the kanji 火 (meaning fire) and 山 (meaning mountain) together you get 火山 which means volcano – a fire mountain!

しゅくだい

HOMEWORK:

Ask your teacher for flashcards for the 5 hiragana you have learnt so far. Colour them in and put them up in your room or on your fridge. Practise reading them every time you see them.

CD ROM

Hey! I can:

- ☐ Talk about the Japanese writing system
- ☐ Recognise examples of hiragana,katakanaandkanji
- ☐ Write 5 hiragana
- ☐ Read 5 greeting words in Japanese

③おなまえは？ What's your name?

On this page you will learn how to ask someone's name and answer when someone asks you. You'll also learn how to write your name in Japanese with a special calligraphy brush, on a Japanese scroll which you've made yourself C'mon, let's get on with it!

NEW STUFF きょうのポイント

Fill in the English meanings.

おなまえは？
o na ma e wa

your name です。
de su

ぼくは Ben です。
bo ku wa de su

わたしは your name です。
wa ta shi wa de su

わたしは Kate です。
wa ta shi wa de su

Milly です。
de su

ぼくは your name です。
bo ku wa de su

"My name is...

Watch the CD-ROM and write down the names of the people introducing themselves.

Then, using the hiragana chart on page 10, try to figure out how to write the names in Japanese.

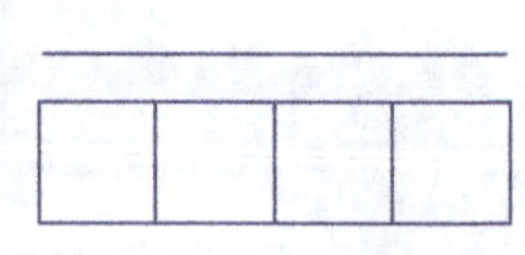

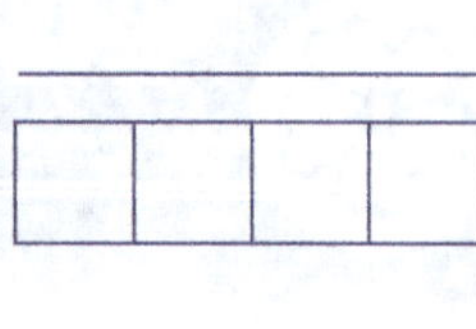

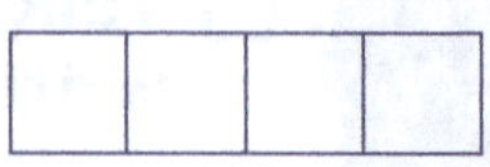

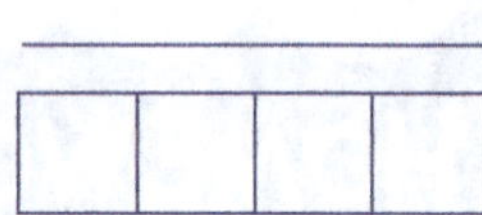

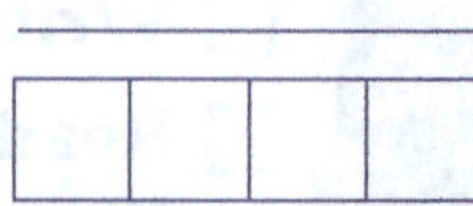

Role-play it

Walk around the class and ask 6 people what their names are and answer when they ask you.

This game involves singing the song, running, noise and tough competition, so be nice to your teacher before you ask to play it!

CD ROM

Hey!

Do you remember about さん*san*, くん*kun* and ちゃん*chan*?...well don't forget to use them. BUT WAIT! NEVER PUT SAN OR KUN ON THE END OF YOUR OWN NAME, ESPECIALLY IF YOU ARE INTRODUCING YOURSELF...you don't need to be polite to yourself!

Find out all about Japanese names on the CD-ROM then have a guess which ones you think are girls' names and which ones you think are boys' names. Check the answers with your teacher, then colour the girls' names pink and the boys' names blue.

CD ROM

XTRA STUFF もっともっと

After you tell someone your name you can say that you are pleased to meet them.

どうぞよろしく I'm pleased to meet you.
do u zo yo ro shi ku

See this conversation on the CD-ROM.

Try a conversation with your friend using the whole pattern:

A こんにちは。
ko n ni chi wa

B こんにちは。
ko n ni chi wa

A わたしは your name です。おなまえは？
wa ta shi wa de su o na ma e wa

B わたしは your name です。どうぞよろしく。
wa ta shi wa de su do u zo yo ro shi ku

A どうぞよろしく。
do u zo yo ro shi ku

Or this one:

A こんにちは。わたしは your name です。おなまえは？
ko n ni chi wa wa ta shi wa de su o na ma e wa

B こんにちは。わたしは your name です。どうぞよろしく。
ko n ni chi wa wa ta shi wa de su do u zo yo ro shi ku

A どうぞよろしく。
do u zo yo ro shi ku

Try and write your own conversation using all of the words you know.

Ai

Sakura

Yuki

Ayumi

Akihiro

Haruna

Makoto

Masao

Tatsuya

Hiroki

Takumi

Kenta

Tomoyasu

Write your name!

If you are not Japanese, your name is written in katakana and is spelt in Japanese how it sounds to the Japanese ear!

Ask your teacher to write your name in Japanese in the squares below, then follow these steps to write your name yourself.

Step 1: Highlight the characters in your name in the katakana chart below.

Step 2: Ask your teacher to check that you have highlighted the correct characters.

Step 3: Write the characters yourself, following the order of the strokes shown in the chart in the inside cover.

Step 4: If you have special characters in your name, like ー, ジ, パ or ones which are written smaller than the others, copy these too.

Practise writing your name 4 times!

Teacher writes here

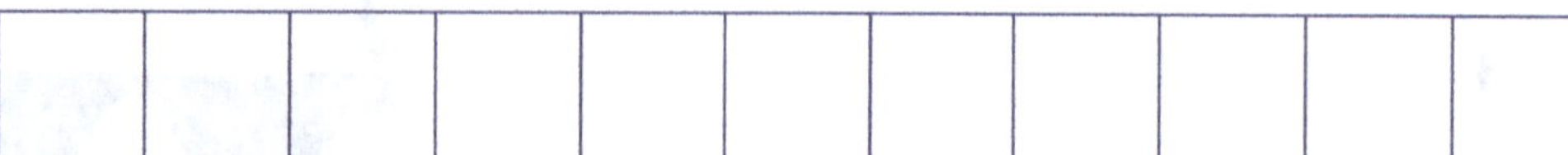

You write here

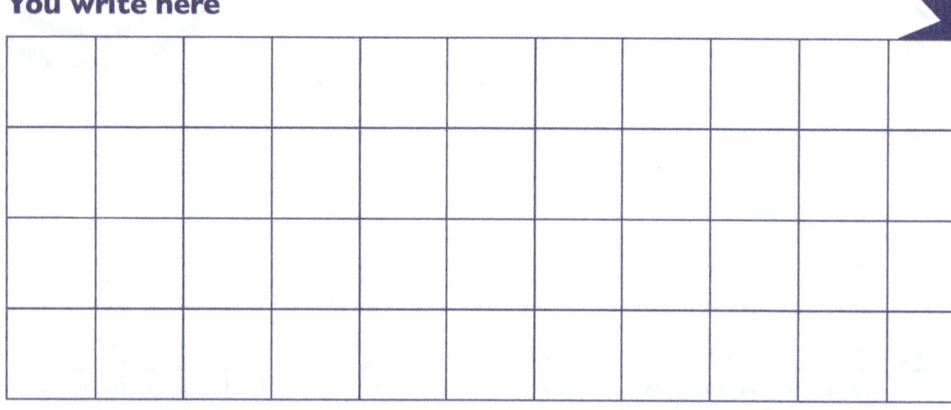

A closer look at Katakana

Check out the katakana chart to be able to write your and your friends' names. Good luck!

	w	r	y	m	h	n	t	s	k		
ン	ワ	ラ	ヤ	マ	ハ	ナ	タ	サ	カ	ア	a
		リ		ミ	ヒ	ニ	チ	シ	キ	イ	i
		ル	ユ	ム	フ	ヌ	ツ	ス	ク	ウ	u
		レ		メ	ヘ	ネ	テ	セ	ケ	エ	e
	ヲ	ロ	ヨ	モ	ホ	ノ	ト	ソ	コ	オ	o

Let's make a kakejiku....a what?.....a kakejiku..........it's a long Japanese hanging scroll with some Japanese writing on it. Ask your teacher if you can get the instructions from the CD-ROM

Ask your teacher for instructions on how to screen print your name on a T-shirt or a pillow case.

Also, check out the website for more on popular names and their meanings.

Not sure?

If you are not sure and want to check someone's name you can say:

(name) さんですか。
sa n de su ka

Are you __________?

You can answer:

はい、(name) です。
ha i de su

Yes I'm (name).

or

いいえ、(name) です。
i i e de su

No, I'm (name).

Practise with the CD-ROM. Then, grab a friend and practise the conversation again.

かなコーナー
Kana Corner

Let's practise writing some new hiragana characters. Make sure you use for the correct stroke order.

na	な	な						
te	て	て						
de	で	で						
su	す	す						

Blind Man's Bluff

Check out the CD-ROM for a game of Blind Man's Bluff in Japanese. Then try it yourself.

On the video the boys used the following expressions:

1. はい、そうです。
ha i so u de su
"Yes, you're right"

2. いいえ、ちがいます。
i i e chi ga i ma su
"No, you're wrong."

You can use them too if you like.

Let's Read!

Read this short dialogue. Write their names in English.

Boy: おなまえは。

Girl: まさこです。 ....

Girl: おなまえは。

Boy: なおやです。 ....

しゅくだい

HOMEWORK:

Practise writing your name in Japanese every day.

1. Make yourself a sign for your bedroom door.

2. Write your name in Japanese on all of your school books.

3. Print out a photo of you and your friends and write your name in Japanese under your photo. Then, ask your friends to show you how to write their names.

CD ROM

Hey! I can:

- ☐ **Ask someone their name**
- ☐ **Say who I am**
- ☐ **Check someone's name if I am not sure**
- ☐ **Write my name in Japanese**
- ☐ **Read the question:** おなまえは？
- ☐ **Write the answer: (my name)** です。

④日本のイメージ Images of Japan

What do you already know about Japan? When you think 'Japan'... what do you see? Grab a group of friends, a thick marker and a large piece of paper, and make a mind map of all of your images of Japan. Write 'Japan' (日本) in the centre of your paper, and in 5 minutes see how many images you can come up with.

Now, check out the CD-ROM for some other images of Japan which you might not have thought of.

CD ROM Japan!

Let's practice writing the kanji for Japan.

ni	日	日					
hon	本	本					

Round 1: What do you know?

What do you already know about life in Japan? Colour in the correct box and for each correct answer you'll get 3 points. There are 3 rounds to go, so get ready.

What language do Japanese people speak?

- ☐ Chinese
- ☐ Japanese

Traditionally, what do Japanese people eat with?

- ☐ Chopsticks
- ☐ Their left hand

What is the first thing that Japanese people do when they enter a house?

- ☐ Take off their shoes
- ☐ Wash their hands

Traditionally, where do Japanese people sleep?

- ☐ On a futon on the floor
- ☐ On a bed with a feather doona

What is the name of the famous Japanese dish consisting of rice and fish or vegetables rolled up in seaweed?

- ☐ Sushi
- ☐ Sashimi

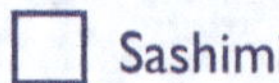

What is the name of the traditional dress of Japan?

- ☐ Kimono
- ☐ Hijab

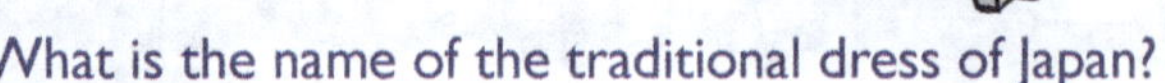

Which of these came from Japan?

- ☐ Xbox
- ☐ Nintendo Gameboy

What food is eaten with most meals?

- ☐ Bread rolls
- ☐ Rice

Check with your teacher, add up your score and write it in the box below.

My score

Round 2: The Google Round

You have approximately 20 minutes to Google the following information and fill in the table.

Your time starts now!

1. Name the four main islands of Japan.
2. What is the approximate population of Japan?
4. What is the capital of Japan?
5. What is the population of Tokyo?
6. Name three other cities in Japan.
7. What is the name of Japan's highest mountain?
8. What is the name of the currency of Japan?
9. Name three products that are made in Japan.
10. Name three Japanese companies.
11. Colour Australia, Japan and New Zealand on the map.
12. Draw the Japanese flag.

TIME'S UP!

Give yourself 1 point for every correct answer

My score

	Japan (日本)	Your country
Islands		
Approximate Population		
Size		
Capital		
Population of Capital		
Three Other Cities		
Highest Mountain		
Currency		
Products Made Here		
Companies		

Round 3: Japanese words

There are many Japanese words which have found their way into the English language. Recognise any of these? Match up each word with its definition by drawing a connecting line. Then check out the answers on the CD-ROM. Give yourself one point for every correct answer.

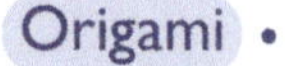

Origami •	• Singing songs through a microphone with words appearing on a screen
Sudoku •	• A game console that plugs into the TV
Ikebana •	• A Japanese martial art
Tofu •	• A Japanese dish of rice rolls wrapped in seaweed containing fish or vegetables
Karaoke •	• A number puzzle originating in Japan
Samurai •	• The Japanese art of paper folding
Karate •	• A Japanese electronics company
Futon •	• A Japanese car company
Nintendo •	• A character and range of merchandise made by Sanrio
Toshiba •	• Raw fish
Hello Kitty •	• A Japanese warrior
Kimono •	• A tidal wave caused by an earthquake
Toyota •	• Flower arranging
Sushi •	• Soya bean curd used in Japanese and vegetarian cooking
Anime •	• A bed on the floor
Tsunami •	• Japanese-style cartoons
Sashimi •	• A Japanese traditional dress

My score

Wonderword team challenge!

There are many Japanese words which have found their way into the English language. Open up the CD-ROM and play the **Wonderword team challenge!**

Form two teams. The teacher will give you a clue to find these familiar Japanese words in the wonderword puzzle. You have to be the first team to find the correct word and give its position on the grid. You get one point for your team if you can. Good Luck!

Gambatte! がんばって！

	a	b	c	d	e	f	g	h	i	j
1	X	X	T	O	F	U	X	X	X	K
2	S	U	S	H	I	S	X	N	X	I
3	X	S	U	X	I	A	T	I	X	M
4	T	A	N	X	K	S	O	N	H	O
5	O	M	A	X	E	H	S	T	E	N
6	Y	U	M	X	B	I	H	E	L	O
7	O	R	I	G	A	M	I	N	L	X
8	T	A	A	X	N	I	B	D	O	X
9	A	I	N	K	A	R	A	O	K	E
10	N	X	I	A	X	X	X	X	I	X
11	I	X	M	R	X	X	X	X	T	X
12	M	X	E	A	X	X	X	X	T	X
13	E	F	U	T	O	N	X	X	Y	X
14	X	X	X	E	S	U	D	O	K	U

CD ROM

かがみコーナー
Kagami Corner

To reveal this info about Japan you will need a かがみ *kagami*, a mirror to help you! Do this task at home and be ready to discuss it in class. Then, check out the photos on the CD-ROM

Shoes off please!

Japanese people never wear shoes inside their houses. They have a small area at the front door before they step up into the house called the げんかん genkan where they leave their shoes. Even if you visit someone else's house you must take off your shoes and leave them there.

Chopsticks or spoon?

Everyone in the family has their own chopsticks. Most Japanese food is eaten with chopsticks including Japanese miso soup. You pick the pieces of meat or vegetable out with your chopsticks and then drink the soup straight from the bowl. Not all food, however, is eaten with chopsticks. Curry rice is eaten with a spoon, cakes are eaten with a fork, desserts with a spoon and sushi can be picked up in your fingers!

Sleeping Quarters

Traditionally, Japanese people sleep on a bed on the floor, called ふとん futon which is folded up and put away in a cupboard, the おしいれ oshiire, in the morning. However, these days many Japanese people sleep on a bed with a doona on the top. You will usually find that futon are used when a guest comes to stay.

おりがみタイム origami Time

Watch the video to see how to make the perfect origami crane. You'll need a piece of paper to work with.

The crane

Speaking about symbols of Japan! The crane is one of them! In Japanese it is called つる (tsuru). The crane is the symbol of long life and peace. Come on, get a piece of paper now and learn how to make an origami crane! You will also find all the instructions in the website, just in case.

You may also want to read *Sadako and the Thousand Paper Cranes* by Eleanor Coerr, a true story about a girl who lived in Japan in the time just after World War II.

おふろ! Bath Time!

Japanese baths are not for washing but for relaxing in. Whether bathing at home or in a public bath, there is a set procedure to follow. First you take off your clothes in a room next to the bathroom and leave them in a basket provided. Then you go into the bathroom and wash yourself thoroughly using a hand shower or bowls of hot water, which you fill up from taps low on the wall. When you are completely clean you hop into the bath, which is filled to the brim with very hot water. You can sit and soak for between 20 and 40 minutes. Japanese people love to visit public baths in some parts of Japan where everyone soaks together in natural hot water from hot springs. But don't worry, boys go in one bath and girls in the other!

What are the rules for having a Japanese bath?

Number the steps.

- ☐ Enter the ふろば furoba
- ☐ Hop in the bath
- ☐ Take off your clothes and leave them in the basket outside the bathroom
- ☐ Wash yourself thoroughly with soap and a small towel
- ☐ Soak in the hot water to relax for about 20 minutes

LET'S Guess!

See if you can name the Japanese things, which are scattered around the page.

Has anyone in your family been to Japan? Maybe they have brought home some souvenirs. If you have anything Japanese at home bring it in and tell the class about it.

しゅくだい

HOMEWORK:

Show and Tell

Flick through magazines or travel brochures and find your own images of Japan. Make them into a collage on an A4 piece of paper and cover it with clear contact or laminate it. They can be pictures, company logos, anime characters or anything Japanese. When you have finished count up the number of images you have found and see who in your class has a found the most. If you are a computer wiz, and would prefer to do a digital collage, that's OK too. You can display them on your classroom wall, then afterwards you can use it as a したじき (*shitajiki*). All Japanese kids use them!

CD ROM

Hey! I can:

- ☐ **Identify popular images of Japan**
- ☐ **Write 日本, which means 'Japan'**
- ☐ **Talk a bit about things Japanese people do in their daily lives**
- ☐ **State some facts comparing Australia and Japan**
- ☐ **Make an origami crane**

⑤どこに住んでいますか？ Where do you live?

Fasten your seat belts! It's time to do a quick tour of Japan and test your knowledge of Australia and New Zealand. But hey! Where do you live?

きょうのポイント

Practise the pattern on the CD-ROM and with your teacher. Then fill in the English meanings:

どこにすんでいますか。 ____________________
do ko ni su n de i ma su ka

place where you live にすんでいます。 ____________________
ni su n de i ma su

More examples:

オーストラリアにすんでいます。 ____________________
o o su to ra ri a ni su n de i ma su

日本にすんでいます。 ____________________
ni hon ni su n de i ma su

ニュージーランドにすんでいます。 ____________________
nyu u ji i ra n do ni su n de i ma su

ブリスベンにすんでいます。 ____________________
bu ri su be n ni su n de i ma su

とうきょうにすんでいます。 ____________________
to u kyo u ni su n de i ma su

オークランドにすんでいます。 ____________________
o o ku ra n do ni su n de i ma su

What kind of writing are the Australian place names written in? Why?

City Names

Cities in Australia

Ask your teacher to say the cities and see if you can guess them in English. Write them in the space provided. Then, check on the CD-ROM if you've guessed them right.

オーストラリア
o o su to ra ri a ____________

ダーウィン
da a wi n ____________

ブリスベン
bu ri su be n ____________

シドニー
shi do ni i ____________

キャンベラ
kya n be ra ____________

メルボルン
me ru bo ru n ____________

ホバート
ho ba a to ____________

アデレード
a de re e do ____________

パース
pa a su ____________

Cities in New Zealand

Ask your teacher to say the cities and see if you can guess them in English. Write them in the space provided. Then, check on the CD-ROM if you've guessed them right.

ニュージーランド
nyu u ji i ra n do ____________

ウェリントン
we ri n to n ____________

オークランド
o o ku ra n do ____________

ロトルア
ro to ru a ____________

クライストチャーチ
ku ra i su to cha a chi ____________

ダニーデン
da ni i de n ____________

What kind of writing are New Zealand place names written in? Why?

Find out from your teacher how to write the name of the place where you live. Copy it into the boxes below.

かなコーナー Kana Corner

Look at the new characters on the CD-ROM and practise writing them here in the correct stroke order.

o	オ	オ							
ni	ニ	ニ							
to	と	と							
do	ど	ど							
ni	に	に							
n	ん	ん							
i	い	い							

International Native Animal Convention

Read the cartoons and answer the following questions

What question does the giraffe ask?

What does the koala answer? ______________________

What does the crane answer? ______________________

What does the kiwi answer? ______________________

おしゃべり タイム
Talk Time

Go around the class and find out where everyone lives. Of course, you'll have to say what suburb you live in instead of what city because all of your classmates live in the same city. Practice with your teacher first. Record the name of the person you asked and the suburb in English in the table provided. Don't forget to ask the questions in Japanese!

おなまえは？ o na ma e wa	どこにすんでいますか。 do ko ni su n de i ma su ka

XTRA STUFF もっともっと

Sometimes you need to make it clear where you live if people are not familiar with your city or country. For example, you can say that you live in Melbourne, Australia. You will link the 2 places with the word の (*no*).

1. Put the bigger one first, (Australia)
2. link with の (*no*)
3. put the smaller one next (Melbourne)
4. then the にすんでいます。 (*ni sunde imasu.*)
5. You will have the whole sentence:

オーストラリアのメルボ
o o su to ra ri a no me ru bo
ルンにすんでいます。
ru n ni su n de i ma su

"I live in Melbourne in Australia"

To say you live in Bondi, in Sydney, you'll use:

シドニーのボンダイに
shi do ni i no bo n da i ni
すんでいます。
su n de i ma su

"I live in Bondi in Sydney."

It's your turn! How would you say

I live in Perth in Australia.

I live in Dunedin in New Zealand.

I live in Osaka in Japan.

I live in Cronulla in Sydney.

Tell the class exactly where you live.

どこにすんでいますか。
do ko ni su n de i ma su ka

CD ROM

Cities in Japan

Japanese place names are written in Kanji. That's because, like Japanese people's names, they mean something. It's sort of like Aboriginal place names in Australia and Maori place names in New Zealand. Some examples:

東京 Tokyo means Eastern Capital

大阪 Osaka means Big Hill

松山 Matsuyama means Pine Tree Mountain

Ask your teacher to say the cities and see if you can guess them in English.

日本	
札幌	さっぽろ sa p po ro
東京	とうきょう to u kyo u
京都	きょうと kyo u to
富士山	ふじさん fu ji sa n
奈良	なら na ra
大阪	おおさか o o sa ka
広島	ひろしま hi ro shi ma
宮島	みやじま mi ya ji ma
松山	まつやま matsu ya ma
長崎	ながさき na ga sa ki

Where do these people live?

Let's revise the names of some Australian cities. If you want to try to read the Japanese, cover up the pronunciation and use the list of Australian cities to figure out where each of these people live. You only need to look at the first character and try to find it in the list.

ブリスベンにすんでいます。
bu ri su be n ni su n de i ma su

ホバートにすんでいます。
ho ba a to ni su n de i ma su

シドニーにすんでいます。
shi do ni i ni su n de i ma su

アデレードにすんでいます。
a de re e do ni su n de i ma su

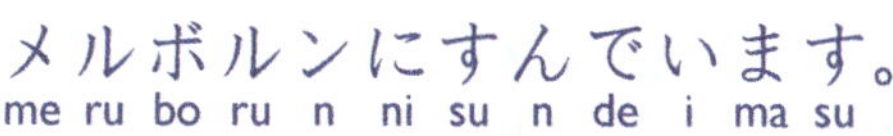

メルボルンにすんでいます。
me ru bo ru n ni su n de i ma su

Listen to the song on the CD-ROM, and then sing along!

ド・レ・ミ・ファ・そんぐ

Sung to the tune of *10 Little Indians*

1

どこにすんでいますか
do ko ni su n de i ma su ka

さっぽろ、とうきょう、おおさか
sa p po ro to u kyo u o o sa ka

ひろしま、みやじま、まつやま
hi ro shi ma mi ya ji ma ma tsu ya ma

にすんでいます。
ni su n de i ma su

2

どこにすんでいますか
do ko ni su n de i ma su ka

シドニー、ブリズベン、ホバート、
shi do ni i bu ri zu be n ho ba a to

パース、メルボルン、アデレード、
pa a su me ru bo ru n a de re e do

キャンベラ、ダーウィンにすんでいます。
kya n be ra da a wi n ni su n de i ma su

3

どこにすんでいますか
do ko ni su n de i ma su ka

オークランド、ロトルア
o o ku ra n do ro to ru a

クライストチャーチ、ダニーデン、
ku ra i su to cha a chi da ni i de n

ウェリントンにすんでいます。
we ri n to n ni su n de i ma su

How well do you know your cities in Japan, Australia and New Zealand?Here's your chance to show your skill. Gather your team, grab a die and some markers and play どこどこすごろく **The Doko Doko Board Game.**

Throw the die and move the number indicated on the die. If you land on or pass a city card you must identify the city on the card from the clues and give the answer in Japanese by saying that you live there: place にすんでいます。(place *ni sunde imasu*). If you get it right, you throw the die again and gain the number of points indicated on the die and you can continue. If you get it wrong, you have to stay on the city card that you got wrong and try again next turn.

Start Here

奈良

- First capital of Japan
- Famous landmark: Todaiji Temple
- Deer walking freely in the parks

に

こ

ニュージーランド

- Largest city of New Zealand's South Island
- Named after Christ Church Cathedral
- Gateway to the Antarctic

オーストラリア

- Capital of Tasmania
- Was established as a penal colony
- 2nd oldest city

お

富士山

- Japan's highest mountain
- Open for climbing in July and August
- Surrounded by 5 lakes

と

オ

京都

- Ancient Capital of Japan
- Many Famous landmarks including Kinkakuji, Ryuanji and Heian Shrine
- Home of the Geisha

日

す

Dunedin

Christchurch

Hobart

オーストラリア

- Capital of Victoria
- Often referred to as the cultural capital of Australia
- Famous for its trams

で

東京

- Capital of Japan
- Fashion centre of Japan
- Home of the Japanese Royal Family

い

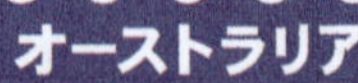

オーストラリア

- Capital of NSW
- Site of Australia's first settlement
- Famous for its Harbour Bridge and Opera House

Find as many hiragana, katakana and kanji as you can hidden in the paths around the island. Colour them in different colours and then copy them in the boxes provided.

オーストラリア

- Capital of South Australia
- Referred to as the city of Churches
- Famous for its wine festivals

札幌

- Largest city in Hokkaido
- Famous for the Snow Festival in February
- Has many hot springs

ニュージーランド

- Second largest city on the South Island
- Origin of the first 'Anzac' biscuit
- Known for tourism and sport

な や さ ま

Adelaide

Sapporo

Nagasaki

Tokyo

Nara

大阪

- 3rd largest city in Japan
- Commercial and industrial centre
- Located in the Kansai region of Japan

ど て ニ

オーストラリア

- Capital of Western Australia
- Located on the Swan River
- Famous for the afternoon sea breeze, known as 'The Fremantle Doctor'

ん

しゅくだい

HOMEWORK:

Research one of the cities in Japan and make a travel brochure.

長崎

- Situated on the island of Kyushu
- Famous for its harbour
- Important city in Japanese history

本

CD ROM

Hey! I can:

- ☐ **Ask someone where they live and answer if someone asks me**
- ☐ **Talk about some cities in Japan, Australia and New Zealand**
- ☐ **Read the Japanese words for Japan, Australia and New Zealand**
- ☐ **Recognise the name in Japanese of the place where I live**
- ☐ **Read the question:** どこにすんでいますか？
- ☐ **Write the answer:** place にすんでいます。

⑥かぞえましょう It all adds up!

Let your teacher know that there is no need to do maths today because we've got it covered. Here, on this page, is all the maths you will need for the whole week. We've covered numbers, time, and space and data. So throw away your maths book, and do it all here. Oh, did I mention that we will be doing it all in Japanese?

Get to 100 in 4 easy steps

Step1:
Learn the numbers 1–10 and practice them.

1	一	ichi
2	二	ni
3	三	san
4	四	yon
5	五	go
6	六	roku
7	七	nana
8	八	hachi
9	九	kyuu
10	十	jyuu

Listen to these guys counting from 1-10. Practise in your class.

Number mousse

Draw your mousse as you make it.

Recipe

You will need:
- The numbers from 1-10
- A deep glass dish
- A wooden spoon

1) Line a dish with number 10s, spreading them to the edges.
2) Spoon in a thick layer of number 3s then a thin layer of number 7s.
3) Put in a layer of number 6s followed by a layer of number 1s.
4) Put a layer of number 5s in one half of the dish and number 2s in the other.
5) Finish with a thick layer of number 9s and then scatter number 8s on the top.
6) Decorate your mousse with dollops of number 4s.

Look on the CD ROM for a song and some actions to do to remember the numbers 1–10

ド・レ・ミ・ファ・そんぐ

The Numbers Song
Here is a way to remember the Japanese numbers from 1 to 10 using actions and a very silly song to the tune of *Do-Ra-Mi*. Do the actions as you sing the song and try to sing the Japanese numbers with the correct pronunciation.

One and two, my **ichi ni**
Three, the **san** up in the sky
Four, a **yon** I'm really bored
go right out the door, bye bye!

roku playing my guitar
Seven **nana** nah nah nah
Eight the rabbit's **hachi** and then
kyuu is nine and **jyuu** is ten

XTRA STUFF もっともっと

You can use the numbers from 1–9 to talk about your phone number. To ask "What is your phone number?" you can say:

でんわばんごうは？
de n wa ba n go u wa

And you can answer:

03-9685-4111 です。
de su

You only need to remember 2 things:

1. Japanese people say the "–" between the numbers. It is pronounced の (*no*). Just like we pause, it sort of splits up the numbers so it's easier to follow.
2. The word for 0 is ゼロ (*zero*).

What's your phone number?

Write your phone number here in numerals, then see if you can say it in Japanese.

Then, ask 5 friends what their phone numbers are in Japanese.

なまえ na ma e	でんわばんごう de n wa ba n go u

Step 2:

Add 'jyuu' to the front to make the teens. Then, listen to numbers 11–20. Practise it in your class.

11	十一	jyuu ichi
12	十二	jyuu ni
13	十三	jyuu san
14	十四	jyuu yon
15	十五	jyuu go
16	十六	jyuu roku
17	十七	jyuu nana
18	十八	jyuu hachi
19	十九	jyuu kyuu
20	二十	ni juu

Step 3:

Add 'ni' to the front to make the twenties:

21	二十一	jyuu ichi
22	二十二	jyuu ni
23	二十三	jyuu san
24	二十四	jyuu yon
25	二十五	jyuu go
26	二十六	jyuu roku
27	二十七	jyuu nana
28	二十八	jyuu hachi
29	二十九	jyuu kyuu
30	三十	san jyuu

Step 4:

Then change it to:

San at the front to make it the 30s
Yon at the front to make it the 40s
Go at the front to make it the 50s
Roku at the front to make it the 60s
Nana at the front to make it the 70s
Hachi at the front to make it the 80s
Kyuu at the front to make it the 90s

40	四十	yon jyuu
50	五十	go jyuu
53	五十三	go jyuu san
64	六十四	roku jyuu yon
75	七十五	nana jyuu go
86	八十六	hachi jyuu roku
97	九十七	kyuu jyuu nana
100	百	hyaku

Kanji Colour

Find all the examples of each kanji and colour them and their corresponding numeral the same colour.

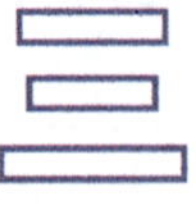

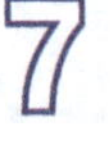

Kanji Corner

Let's learn to write the numbers! First look at the CD ROM and then practise writing the numbers with the correct stroke order.

ichi	一	一						
ni	二	二						
san	三	三						
yon shi	四	四						
go	五	五						
roku	六	六						
nana shichi	七	七						
hachi	八	八						
kyuu	九	九						
jyuu	十	十						

Number Wheels

Complete the number wheel by subtracting the numbers from the number in the centre.

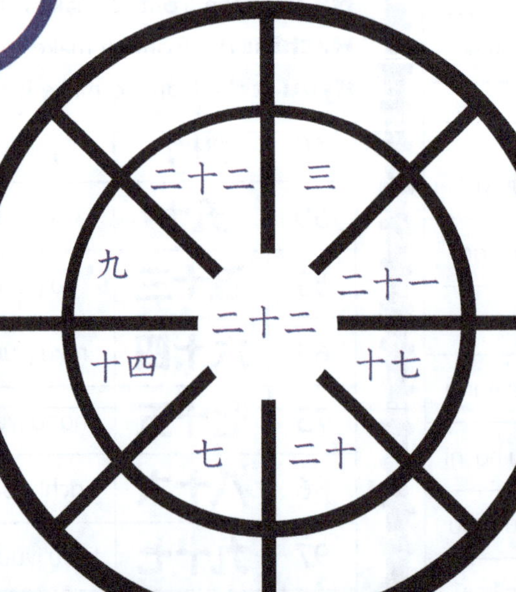

Complete the number wheel by adding the numbers to the number in the centre.

Write true ✓ or false X for each of these statements

九十八 ＞ 八十九 .... ☐

二十五 ＞ 三十二 .... ☐

十六 ＜ 六十 .... ☐

百 ＞ 九 .... ☐

七十四 ＞ 九十三 .... ☐

四十一＞五十八 .... ☐

十二 ＞ 二十一 .... ☐

六 ＜ 四十三 .... ☐

七十五 ＞ 八十五 .... ☐

五十 ＞ 四十八 .... ☐

Hey!

Did you know that Japanese people count to 10 on their fingers using only one hand? Look at the diagram and see if you can do it too.

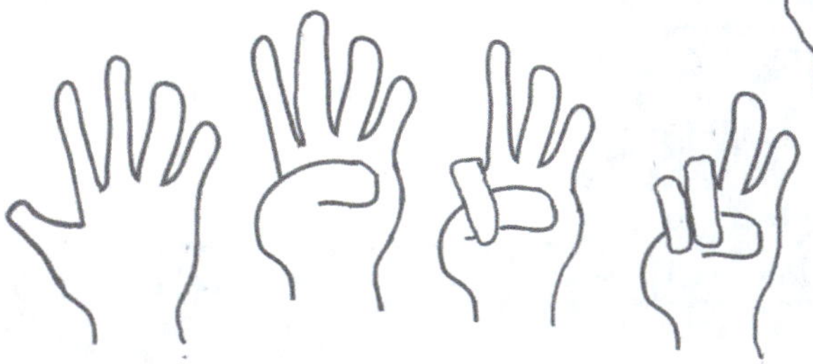

Complete the number sequences

三十二、 三十四、 三十六、 三十八、 ______、 ______、 ______

十、二十、三十、四十、______、______、______

八十、七十五、七十、六十五、______、______、______

三、六、九、十二、______、______、______

二十二、三十、三十八、四十六、______、______、______

九十二、八十八、八十四、八十、______、______、______

Task: Shape up!

How many sides do these shapes have?

☐ ☐

☐ ☐

How many times?

In a typical day how many times do you do these things?

Write the number in Japanese in the box.

Wash your hands? ....

Hear your mum/dad say "Hurry up!" ....

Check your email? ....

Text your friends (this information will remain confidential– we won't tell your parents!)? ....

Hear your mum/dad say "Clean up your room!" ....

Turn on the TV? ....

Eat a piece of fruit? ....

Measure Up

Measure the following objects in your room and write the answer in Japanese. The answer will be in centimetres (センチ) or metres (メートル). Cross out the one that does not apply.

Your desk: ____________ センチ ／ メートル

Your Obento snack pack: ____________ センチ ／ メートル

Your pencil: ____________ センチ ／ メートル

Your favourite book or toy: ____________ センチ ／ メートル

Something stuck to your wall: ____________ センチ ／ メートル

The height of the pile of clothes on your floor! ____________ センチ ／ メートル

Hey! Do you know what this is? It's a soroban. Check the CD-ROM...

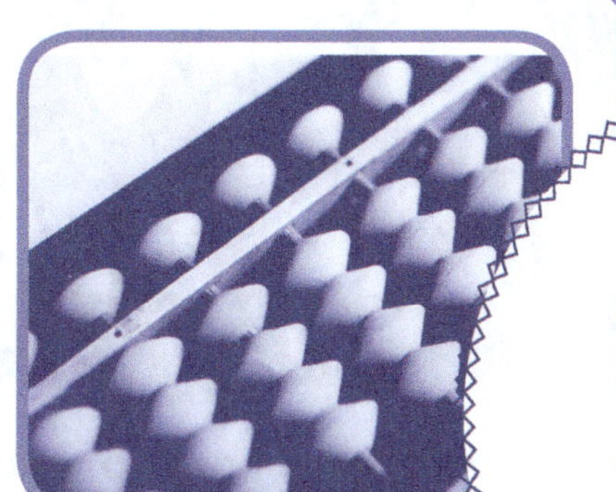

Numbers Team Game Challenge

しゅくだい

HOMEWORK:

Make your dice!

Use the pattern to make your own Japanese die, which you can use to play some games later.

Ask your teacher for a copy of the pattern.

Colour the kanji in your favourite colours.

Glue it to a piece of cardboard (a shoe box or shirt packing is good).

Cut it out.

Fold along the dotted lines, tuck in the tabs and glue it where indicated.

CD ROM

Hey! I can:

- ☐ Count to 100
- ☐ Read and write the numbers from 1–100
- ☐ Ask what someone's phone number is and answer when someone asks me
- ☐ Do all my maths homework in Japanese
- ☐ Understand how a soroban works

⑦ なんさいですか？ How old are you?

Have a look at how to talk about ages so you can play ...

Celebrity Age Gauge Challenge
「なんさいですか」チャレンジ

How well do you know your celebrities?

For a chance to test your knowledge, play the Celebrity Age Gauge Challenge on the website!

NEW STUFF きょうのポイント

Fill in the English meanings and practice these structures on the CD-ROM.

なんさいですか。 ____________
na n sa i de su ka

age さいです。 ____________
sa i de su

九 さいです。 ____________
kyuu sa i de su

十 さいです。 ____________
jyu s sa i de su

十一さいです。 ____________
jyuu i s sa i de su

十二さいです。 ____________
jyuu ni sa i de su

十三さいです。 ____________
jyuusa n sa i de su

Draw a picture of a person who is each of these ages.

八さいです。	九十二さいです。	五十四さいです。
一さいです。	三十五さいです。	十七さいです。

How do you write this?

Try turning these numbers into ages. Write them in Japanese and practice saying them as you write them. The first one has been done for you.

16	十六さい
10	
34	
62	
12	
21	
43	
15	
58	
27	
11	
9	
83	
32	
76	
8	
24	
4	
38	
45	
13	

XTRA STUFF もっともっと

Hey! Check the CD-ROM for some extra stuff. You can put わたしは (*wa ta shi wa*) if you are a girl or ぼくは (*bo ku wa*) if you are a boy on the front of any of the sentences we have learnt so far to emphasize that you are talking about yourself. They mean "I am." Of course you can leave it off, but it's more impressive to put it on.

CD ROM

Using "wa ta shi wa" or "bo ku wa", tell your class your age.

CD ROM

A word on Pronunciation

Generally, it's easy to say your age. You just say さい (*sa i*) at the end of the Japanese number. However, there are a few exceptions which make them easier to say. Here they are, and listen to them on the CD-ROM as well:

1 year old	一さい	いっさい (i s sa i)
8 years old	八さい	はっさい (ha s sa i)
10 years old	十さい	じゅっさい (jyu s sa i)

and therefore:

11 year old	十一さい	じゅういっさい (jyu u i s sa i)
18 years old	十八さい	じゅうはっさい (jyu u ha s sa i)

Hey!

With 20 years old you don't put さい, just the numbers, and it's pronounced はたち. (ha ta chi)

20 years old
二十　はたち

What's my age?

Watch the video footage of the Japanese people telling you their ages. Write them down in numerals as you hear them.

1 ______
2 ______
3 ______
4 ______
5 ______
6 ______

Other ages

Let's repeat all these ages with the CD-ROM! You'll become a super expert!

Age Info:

Different ages are very important in Japanese culture. Find out about it from the CD-ROM and answer these questions.

1a. What ages are celebrated in a special festival held on the 15th of November each year?

____

b. What is the festival called?

____

2. At what age do you become an adult in Japan?

____

3a. When is Coming of Age Day?

____

b. How is it celebrated?

____

4a. What are the bad luck ages for men?

____

b. What are the bad luck ages for women?

____

Celebrity Age Gauge Challenge

「なんさいですか」チャレンジ

Here's your chance to prove your knowledge. It's the Celebrity Age Gauge Challenge! Check out the CD-ROM and in teams, try to work out how old the celebrities are now… and say it in Japanese!

Don't get stuck in the Age Maze!

Follow the ages from 1–20 to get through the maze to adulthood.

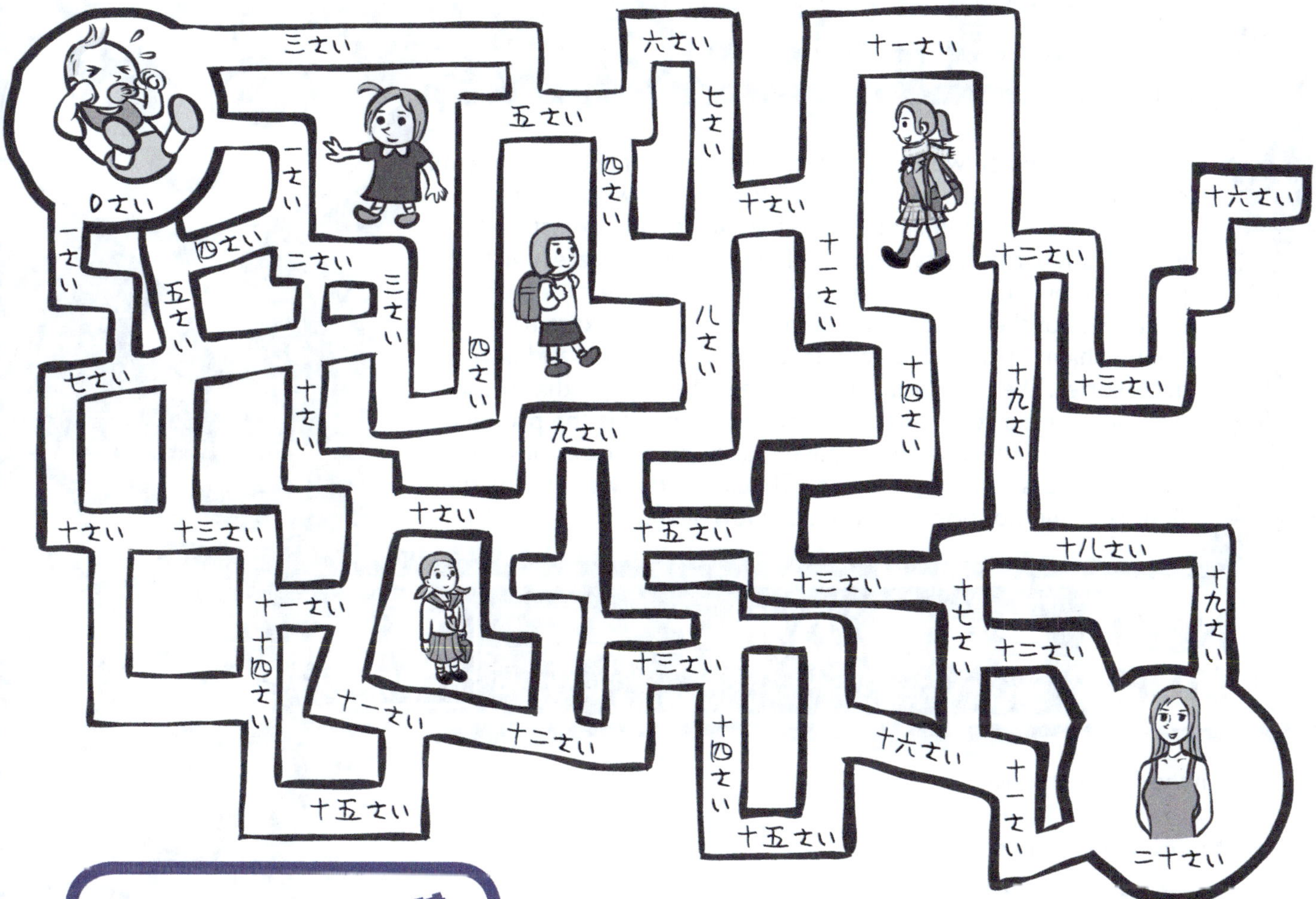

Try the Q&A Game

HOMEWORK:

Write down the ages of each of the members of your family. Teach them how to say their ages in Japanese. Compare the ages of your parents and brothers and sisters with those of your friends.

CD ROM

Hey! I can:

- ☐ Ask someone how old they are and answer if someone asks me
- ☐ Understand when someone tells me how old they are
- ☐ Read the question: なんさいですか？
- ☐ Write the answer: age さいです。
- ☐ Read and write ages up to 100
- ☐ Talk about special celebrations

⑧しゅみはなんですか？ Flash Fads and Hot Hobbies

Traditionally, when we think of Japan we think of kimono, origami cranes, cherry blossoms and sushi. However, now there are anime, Hello Kitty, tamagotchi and the latest and coolest in digital gadgets and gizmos. Japanese kids love to have the latest virtual pet, electronic device or character toy and consider it essential to have all of the associated merchandise from stickers to phone chains, pencil cases and stationery to T-shirts and fashion accessories. The market in Japan is huge. The thing is that these products have a very short life-cycle. No sooner is the product released, than the fashion has passed and the next exciting fad is on TV screens and shop shelves. Check out the website for the flash fads and hot hobbies of the last few years.

NEW STUFF きょうのポイント

Fill in the English meanings

しゅみはなんですか。 ______________________
shu mi wa na n de su ka

しゅみは hobby です。 ______________________
shu mi wa de su

hobby です。 ______________________
de su

しゅみはおんがくです。 ______________________
shu mi wa o n ga ku de su

しゅみはコンピューターです。 ______________________
shu mi wa ko n pyu u ta a de su

しゅみはりょうりです。 ______________________
shu mi wa ryo u ri de su

Hey!

If you have two or more hobbies you can use the word と which means '**and**' to say them all. Look at the example:

しゅみ は スポーツ と おんがく です。
shu mi wa su po o tsu to o n ga ku de su

My hobbies are sports and music.

More NEW STUFF きょうのポイント

Watch the video, and fill in the English meanings

activity がすきです。
ga su ki de su

____

テニス がすきです。
te ni su ga su ki de su

____

ギター がすきです。
gi ta a ga su ki de su

____

ゲーム がすきです。
ge e mu ga su ki de su

____

しゅみはスポーツです。サッカー がすきです。
shu mi wa su po o tsu de su sa k ka a ga su ki de su

____

たんご

Words you might need:

Listen these hobbies first. Then, highlight the ones that apply to you. Ask your teacher for any others that you would like to say.

スポーツ sport
su po o tsu

サッカー soccer
sa k ka a

バスケットボール basketball
ba su ke t to bo o ru

スケートボード skate boarding
su ke e to bo o do

テニス tennis
te ni su

ネットボール netball
ne t to bo o ru

ホッケー hockey
ho k ke e

スキー skiing
su ki i

サイクリング bike riding
sa i ku ri n gu

サーフィン surfing
sa a fi n

やきゅう baseball
ya kyu u

じゅうどう judo
jyu u do u

すいえい swimming
su i e i

うた singing
u ta

ピアノ piano
pi a no

ギター guitar
gi ta a

おんがく music
o n ga ku

ダンス dancing
da n su

りょうり cooking
ryo u ri

どくしょ reading
do ku sho

コンピューターゲーム
ko n pyu u ta a ge e mu
computer games

プレステ PlayStation
pu re su te

ゲームボーイ Game Boy
ge e mu bo o i

What's my hobby?

Listen to these boys telling you about their hobbies. Circle the word as you hear it, and write the number of the item next the picture.

やきゅう
ya kyu u

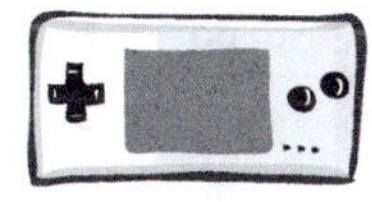

サッカー
sa k ka a

ゲームボーイ
ge e mu bo o i

じゅうどう
jyu u do u

What is that?!?

What do these sentences say? Use the list of hobbies to help you.

1. しゅみ は なんですか。
shu mi wa na n de su ka

2. しゅみ は スポーツ です。バスケットボール が すき です。
shu mi wa su po o tsu de su ba su ke t to bo o ru ga su ki de su

3. しゅみ は おんがく です。うた が すき です。
shu mi wa o n ga ku de su u ta ga su ki de su

4. しゅみ は コンピューター です。プレステ が すき です。
shu mi wa ko n pyu u ta a de su pu re su te ga su ki de su

5. しゅみ は どくしょ です。Harry Potter が すき です。
shu mi wa do ku sho de su ga su ki de su

Off to Camp Shumi!

Fill in the Activity Preference Form by numbering the activities 一 to 二十 in the order that you like them. If you want a challenge, cover up the pronunciation and use the word list to check the activities. Use the trick of just looking at the first character to identify the word. Then, use the tally column to find out the most popular hobby in the class.

Hey! Did you know that instead of using 4 strokes and a cross through it to tally up numbers like we do, Japanese people use a kanji with 5 strokes which looks like this: 正. So each one of these represents 5 counts. Try it when you are tallying up the votes.

しゅみ	preference	tally	しゅみ	preference	tally
プレステ pu re su te			すいえい su i e i		
ギター gi ta a			うた u ta		
スポーツ su po o tsu			どくしょ do ku sho		
サッカー sa k ka a			ピアノ pi a no		
おんがく o n ga ku			ネットボール ne t to bo o ru		
テニス te ni su			スケートボード su ke e to bo o do		
ホッケー ho k ke e			サーフィン sa a fi n		
スキー su ki i			やきゅう ya kyu u		
コンピューターゲーム ko n pyu u ta a ge e mu			ダンス da n su		
サイクリング sa i ku ri n gu			ゲームボーイ ge e mu bo o i		

かなコーナー
Kana Corner

Look at the new hiragana characters on the CD-ROM and practice writing them here in the correct stroke order.

shi	し	し						
yu	ゆ	ゆ						
mi	み	み						
ki	き	き						

Shumi charades

Ask the question:

しゅみはなんですか？
shu mi wa na n de su ka

Act out your answer. The rest of the class needs to guess your hobby and answer in Japanese.

Fill in the blanks with your own hobby then try writing the whole sentence in the boxes provided. Either copy the characters or spell it out in letters.

しゅみは＿＿＿＿＿です。
shu mi wa ＿＿＿＿＿ de su

＿＿＿＿＿がすきです。
＿＿＿＿＿ ga su ki de su

Mystery Shumi

Use the pictures to work out each of the *shumi*. Then put together the circled letters to reveal the mystery *shumi*. Write it in the spaces below.

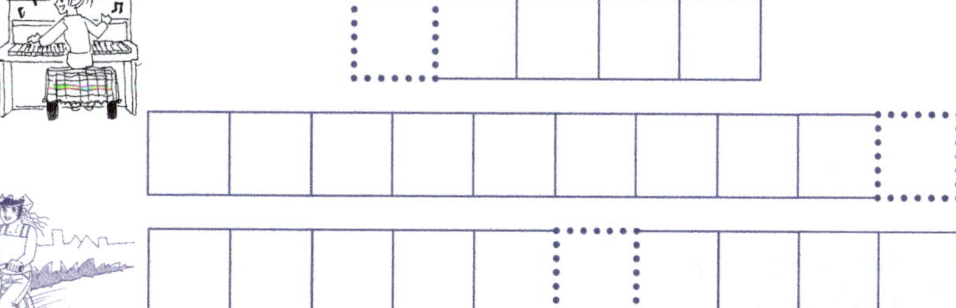

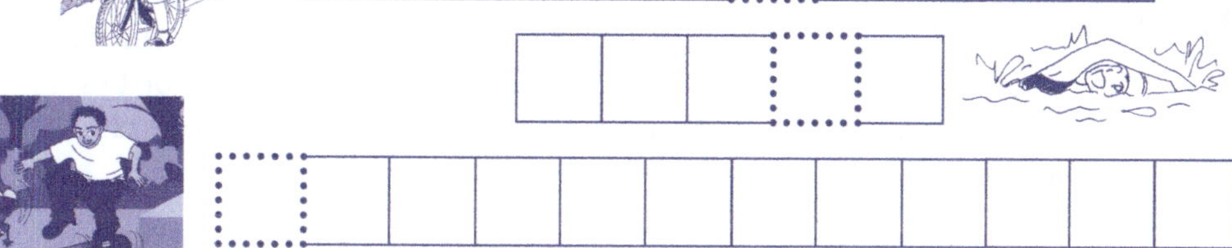

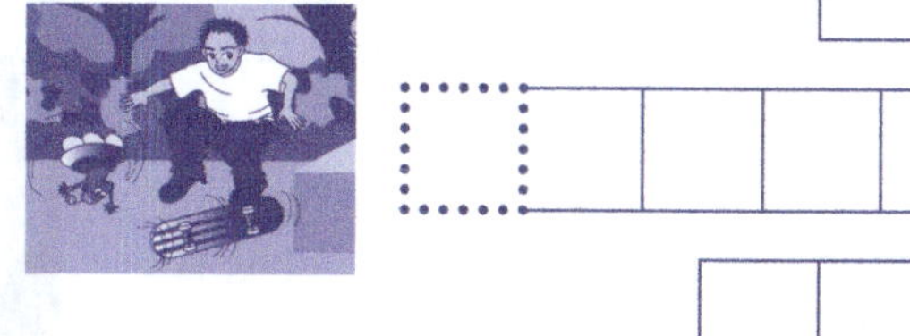

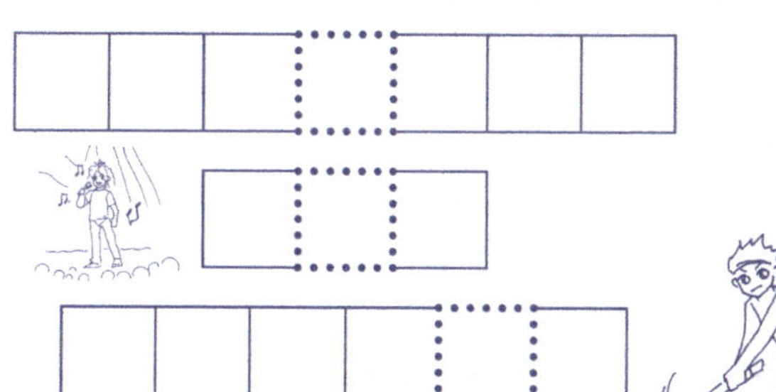

The mystery *shumi* is

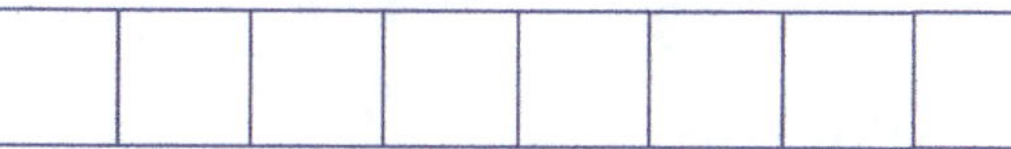

Talk Time おしゃべりタイム

Conduct a class survey in Japanese to find out the most popular hobbies in your class.

Appoint:

- an interviewer to ask the question:

  しゅみはなんですか？
  shu mi wa na n de su ka

- 2 data recorders to record the findings on the board.
- a panel of statisticians to analyse the results.
- the rest of the class to answer the question

Use the last column of the camp shumi form above as your tally sheet and tally up the votes for each hobby as you hear people answer.

Find out the most popular hobby amongst

the boys

the girls

CD ROM

けいたいでんわ Mobile phones

Not a fad, rather, a necessity of life! Everyone from the smallest primary schooler to the oldest *obaasan* and *ojiisan* (grandma and grandpa) seem to carry a *keitai*… and they use it not only for making calls but for a whole heap of other things like: instant messaging, checking train times and service information, electronic money and ticketing, videos and even TV and radio. There is no excuse for missing your favourite show in Japan! You can even connect to a website by simply taking a photo of a special barcode called a QR Code which appears on advertisements and merchandise packaging.

Phone Accessories けいたいのアクセサリー

It's not enough just to have a phone in Japan, you have to have the full range of phone fashion accessories as well! For example, The first thing you need is ストラップ *sutorappu*, a phone strap, with danglies attached with your favourite cartoon or Disney character or traditional lucky charm which not only decorates your phone but also makes it easier to carry.

The next must have is メールブロック (*meeruburokku*), a transparent cover to go over the screen of your phone, which stops anyone reading your messages over your shoulder in a crowded train or public place.

And finally you can decorate your phones with stickers and *purikura*, sticker photos of you and your friends.

Check out some websites for more news about けいたいでんわ (*keitaidenwa*)

Japanese Hobbies

Japanese people might have some different hobbies from those mentioned above. They might like:

けんどう
ke n do u
kendo

カラオケ
ka ra o ke
karaoke

プリクラ
pu ri ku ra
making photo stickers

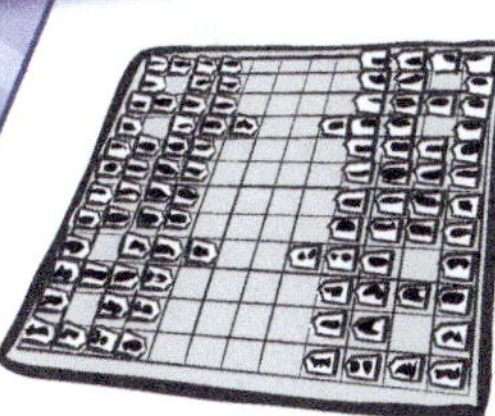

しょうぎ
sho u gi
Japanese chess

いけばな
i ke ba na
flower arrangement

Check out the CD-ROM for more information.

しゅくだい

HOMEWORK:

Jump on the Kids Web Japan website **http://web-japan.org/kidsweb/index.html** and find out about the latest fads and hobbies which are popular in Japan now. Choose one that interests you and prepare a four-page PowerPoint presentation on it. You can include information and, of course, photos. You can even make up a quiz for your friends to do at the end.

Hey! I can:

- ☐ **Ask someone what their hobbies are and answer when someone asks me**
- ☐ **Say what activity I like**
- ☐ **Talk about popular and traditional hobbies**
- ☐ **Read the question:** しゅみはなんですか。
- ☐ **Write the answer:** hobby です。
- ☐ **Read and write a sentence about what I like:** activity がすきです。

Milly's MySpace

HOME | BROWSE | SEARCH | MAIL | BLOG | FAVOURITES | FORUM

Read Milly's MySpace profile and draw a set of pictures that illustrate what Milly has written about herself.

Milly

About Me

こんにちは。ミリー です。十一さい です。
ko n ni chi wa mi ri i de su jyu u i s sa i de su

オーストラリア の シドニー に すんでいます。
o o su to ra ri a no shi do ni i ni su n de i ma su

しゅみ は スポーツ と おんがく です。
shu mi wa su po o tsu to o n ga ku de su

ホッケー と ダンス が すき です。
ho k ke e to da n su ga su ki de su

どうぞよろしく。
do u zo yo ro shi ku

Photos

Milly's MySpace

HOME | BROWSE | SEARCH | MAIL | BLOG | FAVOURITES | FORUM

Now, use Milly's MySpace as a pattern and fill in the blanks to create your own MySpace profile. Attach some photos of yourself in the boxes provided.

About Me

こんにちは。__________です。______さい　です。
ko n ni chi wa　de su　sa i　de su

__________の　__________に　すんでいます。
no　ni　su n de i ma su

しゅみ　は　__________と　__________です。
shu mi wa　to　de su

__________と　__________が　すき　です。
to　ga　su ki　de su

どうぞよろしく。
do u zo yo ro shi ku

Photos

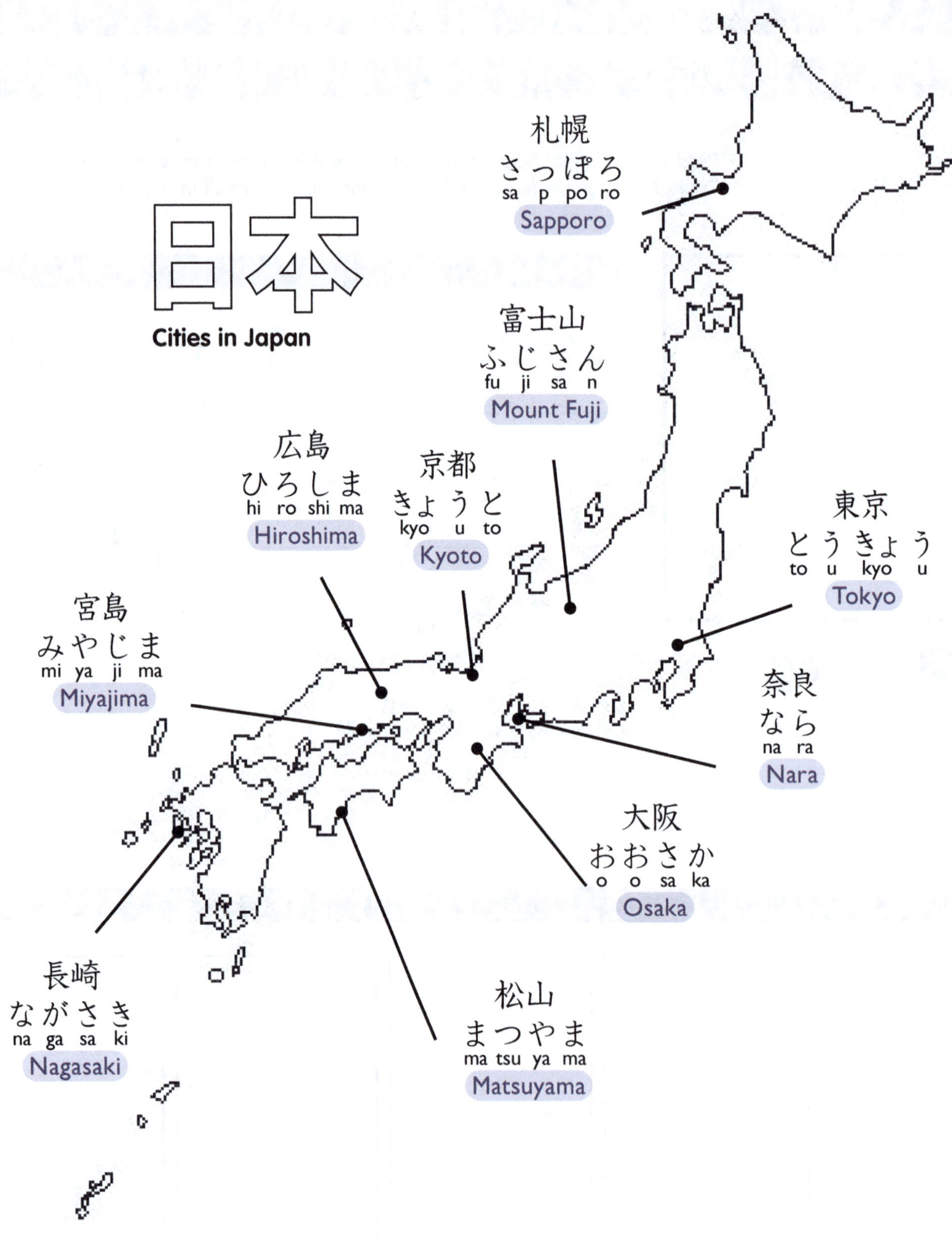
日本
Cities in Japan
札幌
さっぽろ
sa p po ro
Sapporo
富士山
ふじさん
fu ji sa n
Mount Fuji
広島
ひろしま
hi ro shi ma
Hiroshima
京都
きょうと
kyo u to
Kyoto
東京
とうきょう
to u kyo u
Tokyo
宮島
みやじま
mi ya ji ma
Miyajima
奈良
なら
na ra
Nara
大阪
おおさか
o o sa ka
Osaka
長崎
ながさき
na ga sa ki
Nagasaki
松山
まつやま
ma tsu ya ma
Matsuyama

Note

Note